If I Could Speak...

M. J. Vargas

NEBURION
APEX

If I Could Speak…

Copyright © 2026 by Michael Vargas

All rights reserved.

Publisher: Neburion Apex

St. Petersburg, FL

ISBN:

Hardcover: 979-8-9941907-0-8

Cover Design:

Neburion Apex

Interior Layout:

Neburion Apex

Printed in the United States of America

First Edition

Dedication

For those of you who continue to hold it all in. Remember that you matter, remember that what you feel is real. It's acceptable to be selfish and find peace for yourself. Go ahead and conquer the world.

Table of Contents

ACT III: THE ROAD AHEAD

ACT I:

THE FALL

If being crazy means to find uniqueness, then allow me to be the lunatic who isn't scared to go for it.

Devils?

Are we all devils,
in this city of angels,
perplexed by the riches of the few.

Fascinated by the obscurities in the dark,
captured by the sight of monsters lurking among us.

We hide behind our books,
convene with those of our likeness,
speak judgment to those who don't relate.

Does speaking the good word,
absolve us of who we are?

Is it right to use those words as weapons?

To punish others,
in hope to cling on to our power.

Are we all devils?

Or are we all running away from the truth,
that we are no better than the other side.

Ghost

You ever thought what it may be like to be a ghost,
traveling.

Traveling through time,
just watching everything,
wither away in front of your eyes.

What would you feel?

What would you do?

Does your curiosity dissolve,
with the fact that your loved ones would miss you?

Well, I feel like a ghost already,
a living breathing ghost.

Conflicted Love

Lord help me.

Shine bright,
glow far,
impossible to see.

Your breathe is warm,
your arms behold.

The Earth erupts,
the sky dissolves.

Anguish in the air.

Violence on the ground,
impossible to push away.

Impossible but probable,
ignorance like the sharp knife in your tongue.

Language like animals in the rainforest,
rainforest with no man.

Rain with blood,
forest from lies.

Blaspheme,
the middle name of us all.

Blame, blame you, blame me.

Wait and die,
no wait and drown.

Shake your head,
it doesn't stop,
shouts like a giant.

The giant,
the size of the galaxy,
a galaxy without stars.

The stars,
they shine,
darkness awakens,
go away and find yourself.

Yourself,
nasty like garbage,
garbage smells like roses,
roses sting like the devil.

Devil here it is,
go away,
there's nothing else for you to take.

Take away your own curses,
curse like a mule.

Pull yourself together,
it's okay this is it,
you're a mess who needs to rest,
in my arms you will yell for help.

Help will come when you speak the words,
words must be filled with actions,
actions must be done with love,
love must be given to her.

She must be engulfed by you,
and you will be delivered.

It's okay, it's okay,
we are all animals,
we are all fools,
we are all dying lambs,
we are all regretful but look high.

You are special,
special with the serenity of life.

I will write the words of which you will become,
like a mason,
I will make a weapon as beautiful as a nebula,
like Orion's Belt,
I will keep you close to me,
like the sky you will be vast,
and like the stars you will light the way for others.

Close your eyes,
hear me now,

feel me now,
it's okay,
your destroyed,
your lifeless,
but here's life,
here's serenity,
here's the stars and the moon in your hands,
hold on,
hold your breath my love.

I will come to you in the form of your dreams,
in the form of your tears,
in the form of your success,
in the form of your marriage,
I will come my love,
take this knife and take this poison,
but unlike Romeo and Juliet,
throw them in the face of your disgusting difficulties,
in the face of your fears,
in the face of your obstacles,
and take a deep breathe.

I know your crying,
I know your about to fall,
don't go,
come here I will take you to my far away land.

Forever.

The Mind

In the beginning,
mankind had no enemy.

Loud cries covered the land,
peace no one could remember.

How little are our minds?

Minds that hunger with desires,
minds that feed off our emotions.

Like the dawn,
the mind stays stuck between right and wrong.

Struggling to come to a compromise.

We wish to satisfy the mind,
with a temptation that festers,
a temptation that can only be challenged.

Peace to many means having no worries,
about or not having anything critical to think about.

But to what extreme measure,
does the mystery of the mind go to.

Many call the mind our biggest enemy,
fighting away the truth that God wishes to show us.

However, the mind is a part of us,
so wouldn't that make us our own biggest enemy.

The mind tries to find bliss,
in places where the soul bleeds tears of pain and agony,
because while the mind seeks out pleasure in sin,
the soul seeks out comfort in love.

If the mind can't be trusted,
then can we be trusted.

Can we really be trusted in making our own decisions,
if our mind can be deceiving,
or will we wonder in this big field of decisions,
looking for the right one,
like a lost boy looking for his mother.

War

Pick it up.

Pick your weapon.

Go ahead and walk.

You are going to anyways.

Put on your armor,
but wait make sure it fits.

Pick your post,
make sure you become an expert on it.

He is going to be your enemy as well,
yes, that person you call a friend.

Acquaintances, friends, family,
you name it.

They are all a part of it.

These walls can't shy away the truth hidden,
within the belly of the beast.

This hunger for power and acceptance,
it has a nasty resemblance to Cleopatra.

You walk among your enemies like a Judas,
however, you have the disgusting shame,
to keep smiling even after stabbing their backs.

Then again, who is to say,
that they aren't willing to hang you on a tree,
and feed you to wolves.

You make alliances,
you make pacts,
but let's face it,
you are still a warrior in this war,
and at the end it's either you, or them.

We are all in a war,
each with their own army.

The war will go on forever until there is nothing left.

You against everyone,
everyone against you,
everyone against everyone.

We are all in a war,
the final war.

This is it,
this is our last remnant.

Puppet

I break and I break.

These demons inside my chest.

How could you evade?

The truth is too hard to bare.

I took on these shadows with no conscious in vain.

They laugh,
while their heads hang from these ceilings that cave.

Skyscrapers in sight,
tearing them down,
impossible even with all your might.

Run,
run until this wind knocks you off.

A puppet to this world,
or a servant to the Lord.

Must be color deficient to even know the difference.

I lie and I wake,
grabbing this world by the neck to give it a shake.

These demons they surround me playing Russian roulette,
waiting for who will be the lucky one to smack me in the face.

Who called them here,
well I did.

It was either me,
or my family,
well that was an easy choice.

They're my best friends,
because they're the only ones who decide to stay.

Everyone else sees a mistake,
they see a disgrace.

They see no friend in sight,
just another one who isn't worth their sight.

Can't believe all I've given to this world,
still no end in sight.

I'm the monkey in the middle,
taking all the blows they wish to throw.

Might be a homicide,
maybe even a genocide.

Heart torn in pieces,
but truth is all I need is peace.

Could care less of any of your opinions,
I'll stand tall unlike all you minions.

Right and Wrong

Indescribable but in tune,
like the cycles of the moon.

Fear creeps with fire and onyx,
the sweet sound of these harmonics.

Ain't no way it's a lie,
with these feelings that are mine.

This masked beast that's inside,
I wish someone could oblige.

I hate sin,
but my past makes my head spin.

Can't believe I invited an angel to this house I built,
if she is tainted that'll be a heavy guilt.

I hope this is God that I hear,
you are a treasure to me, my dear.

So close, yet so far away.

I'm stuck between doing the right thing the wrong way,
and doing the wrong thing the right way.

You

Let me make this clear,
I put on my gear,
you say that I'm weird,
I call you my dear.

You blow in my face,
give me some space,
look at my face,
I've fallen from grace.

This isn't about you,
you give me the flu,
spit out this stew,
I've got a breakthrough.

Why don't you go,
I don't hate you though,
just want you to know,
I'm tired of you putting me low.

Hell in a cell,
it's your name that I yell,
throw me in jail,
all I see is regrets in this trail.

You found me so lonely,
stayed with me closely,
you looked for a trophy,
charged my anger like a *Mophie*.

Blame

You can be lifted,
if you're just willing.

Ability to be shifted,
to make life thrilling.

The mind keeps pacing,
wondering about life and death.

You just keep pacing,
stop to take a breath.

Betrayal with a kiss,
belief of not having an option.

You dream of sinful bliss,
with no sight of a simple potion.

Stuck in an eternal fight,
pushed to pick a side.

Shaking with all your might,
consumed by the ocean tide.

Just take a break,
before you're burned by the flame.

No reason to feel so fake,
you're not the one to blame.

Regret

To quote *"Schrodinger's Cat"*,
without any concern,
is to imagine a world without consequences.

Without any sort of possible downfall,
like looking down the edge of a hill,
thinking that a fall will make you fly.

For those of us,
looking up high at the top,
we live in obscurity of the possibilities of probabilities.

Maybe we are the cat.

Did the cat get a choice in the situation?

Should we just submit?

To the solace that we find,
in the blissful fear we wear as an armor?

Or should we realize,
that an award without sacrifice,
is like a lethal injection,
of numbing regret.

The Hole

Woe is he,
who has found their hole,
to stem the overreaching roots,
unable to move anymore.

He who can go from hole to hole,
no matter how many times they are cut down,
should embrace the silver lining in the sky.

To be good at all things,
but not be great at one thing is a curse I most fear.

The anguish of being the only flavor of juice left in the aisle.

The last petal to fall,
the last player to be picked.

Yes, you can simply bench the gifts,
you have oh-so ever felt inside,
but in the ring,
fairness is not a matter of whether you win or lose,
it's whether you lift and swing.

They say the criminals come out at night,
to lay waste on the grounds that have been built,
but needless to say, the criminals come out in the day as well,
to take everything in front of you.

Don't jail the criminal,
they swung,
you just didn't like it.

The envy surrounding your eyes strikes with pressure,
unlike Picasso you aren't color blind.

Sure, a man who is taught to fish could feed themselves,
for years to come,
but a man with a fishing pole and no lessons is doomed.

Yes, to ask and be given can become an indulging embrace of
sweet nectar.

Unfortunately, succumbing to this can only place a vial to the
decay you gladly accepted.

Breathe

My feet walk on this ground without soil.
I can't see my hands in this light.

And I breathe.

The air stolen from my chest,
it's a dream.

Do you care to disappear with me?

And I breathe.

Riveting eyes they look upon me now with disbelief.

Do you care to disappear with me?

And I breathe.

These waterfalls brake through my corneas while I scream.

Do you care to disappear with me?

And I breathe.

The highways of regret,
they spiral around my head,
everyone is still bed.

Do you care to disappear with me?

And I breathe.

This pretzel knot inside my chest,
they can't feel what I feel,
so they accumulate these fears that surround me.

Do you care to disappear with me?

And I breathe.

This heart that you gave to me,
is a complicated piece of art from a tragically shattered artist.

Do you care to disappear with me?

And I breathe.

Every time I call your name,
it's the shame that sits deep in,
that won't allow me to forget,
how many times I have disappointed you.

Do you care to disappear with me?

And I breathe.

This place you've brought me to,
there's an angel in this place,
is she a victim or is she prey?

Please don't let me run this one to the ground.

To continue walking on this Earth,
at least one should understand,
that my heart is more than just chambers of pumping veins,
my tears are nothing to fear.

Could you please guide me to the one that will stay?

That will stay because I love them,
no flaw in sight,
just a man who has this weight,
protect them with my faith,
realize them of my shame.

This isn't a man that will run away,
instead claw himself,
to where no one believed he could go.

I'm ashamed to say,
that I have broken these ties between us,
let me be near you to warm myself,
from the cold of this world.
and I breathe one last time.

The End

The end.

We speculate, we contemplate.

The end of this, the end of our lives.

The end of the race, the end of the road.

The end of this fight.

The end of that so called hope,
that one day everything will be better,
and steal away your grief like a thief in the night.

So, you learn from your mistakes,
does that mean your forgiven?

Does being forgiven mean that it never happened?

If it never happened, does that mean that the memory goes
away?

And if the memory goes away,
can you smile once more?

Can forgiveness really become a time machine?

Or will forgiveness forever be that collection of China,
which we hide in that secret door under our feet?

Look at yourself in the mirror,
what do you see?

Do you see a halo,
or horns?

What will you do next with this person that you call,
self?

Murder in your own heart.

You should be ashamed.

The sound of your name should make you bleed,
from your ears.

However, you hear that?

The faint cry of the real person inside of you,
that you have been choking,
with all your distasteful desires and inhumane actions.

So, once again the real question comes to play,
what will you do before the end gets here?

ACT II:

THE AWAKENING

I am far reaching, the Goliath of my story, let David bask in my defeat.

Ocean Heart

Mine heart is an ocean,
deep, conflicted, polluted by the evils of man.

Thy heart is a fragile China on the edge of its demise.

What will thou do if thy China floats on my waters?

Will thou flee along with unspoken words,
or will thou float?

And allow my waters to guide you,
to where thou have never gone.

Mine heart is a delicate ocean,
crying for healing of thy heart.

Dear Lord

Dear Lord,
take this burden from my heart,
take it up to the sky,
let it fall upon me if you really think that I could handle it.

No pain,
no gain,
but my veins feel like hot fire under my skin.

I hope my next kin won't feel their world crumble on them
without warning.

Can't tell left from right,
up from down,
right from wrong,
love from hate,
smiles from frowns.

My intentions are as clear as black and white,
but why does it feel like their hiding in the shadows,
like these devils who want to drown me in this world.

Where do I go?

What do I say?

Why does it feel like looking for love is a grave mistake?

I want to take this mask off,
show everyone who is hiding behind it,
but to them either one looks the same.

Please don't let me just be a shadow,
I don't want to be held back,
by all this darkness that scares me.

I just want to understand these feelings that creep unto me.

Fate

Can't believe this is fate,
I feel like forgotten bait.

Separated from my mate,
it has nothing to do with hate.

Now I'll just have to wait,
for someone to open this gate.

I let go of this heavy weight,
my chest is about to inflate.

I can't even concentrate,
my world is about to detonate.

These eyes cause me to alienate,
these tears that I wish to break,
and find a reason to appreciate,
this world that causes me to asphyxiate.

Little Figure

This eccentric little figure,
dancing around those weeds without soil.

Dancing without eyes,
replaced his eyes for jewels.

The paper doll on the floor,
even more beautiful than when it was high on the pedestal.

Oh!

Woe is this little figure with dreams of love,
but actions of devils.

Great sorrow to this precious paper doll,
who latches on to this little figure.

Tears fall like meteors from the sky.

Oh!

Small figure ignite your rituals in flames,
and feed the ashes to the dogs.

Protect your paper doll from this terrible inferno
and when the rain comes,
you will both stand,
as gold in the middle of the debris.

Mistakes

It keeps creeping back in.

Like a shadow just following me around waiting to strike.

No matter how much noise is around,
it's so quiet.

Am I purposely hurting myself?

Did I jump into this abyss on purpose?

Can God save me?

My hearts rips out of my chest,
a loud cry,
pulsating heat runs through my veins with excruciating pain.

The tears I can't hold in,
the guilt it weighs me down.

Earth and Moon crash,
like football players in a clash.

I bang on this ground,
hollow as this body that I creep in.

Please pick me up with ease.

My knees buckle,
blood spills from these red knuckles.

Tears run down my cheeks while I scream in fear.

Bound by an oath that I beat down to the ground.

Heart is locked to eyes that look like fine art.

Breathing gets harder with time,
when will I reach the ceiling.

God forgive this mess that I've become.

A rotten animal I've become,
I wish I could run.

Don't fall in love with me.
you will hate this break that I'll make,
when I take your fate,
run it to the ground with a rake.

How can I ask for someone to understand my heart,
when I don't understand it myself?

Take this burden that I face,
take me to a place without mistakes.

Cloud

I am as these puffs of air floating in the sky,
growing bigger to intimidate those around you,
shrinking when no one is looking.

People run away on the dark gray days,
ignorant as they come on the bright days.

Is this trajectory my own,
or is the breeze my guide?

Could my mystery be as complex as the shadow I cast?

Unless the substance inside is just as empty as it feels.

Evolve

You drive a Mercedes,
I see you with hades.

Hold off the gravy,
I'm joining the navy.

The future is bleak,
prepared to be meek.

Holding my head up,
I'm cleaning my makeup.

I'm done with this mockery,
it isn't a lottery.

Real lives involved,
need my mind evolved.

Enough

After all these years,
you still fail to see the gears,
that release these tears.

You refuse to look in the mirror,
so you fail to see clearer.

I'll admit I am the villain,
but you are far from a hero.

You can't trust my words,
I can't trust you with my heart.

I'll be made out to be a felon,
it'll be the hole that I fell in.

After this you'll still have your family,
while I go home without the flattery.

I hope you give me some grace,
while you still walk away with all we had,
you'll be taking away the only things I have.

I hope you know I hold no hatred.

I still care,
more than I can bare.

I'll sit alone in this chair,
regardless of whether it's fair.

The loneliness will keep me company,
but I'll be sure to find my peace.

You and Me

Destruction in the midst,
hold your breath and let me blitz.

You see a monster without grit,
can't you see that I've been bit.

This venom belongs here,
with the beauty of your long hair.

Hypnotized by this long stare,
I wish I was there.

A jewel,
hiding,
crying,
sighing,
in the middle of all the artificial smiling.

Perfection has no best friends,
I feel like a mess again.

This could bloom into love,
so let it fly like a dove.

Between you and me there is a guard,
I won't lie this will be hard.

Timing is everything,
so let me be your everything.

I can make all this time feel endless,
but I don't want to scare you by being overzealous.

Beauty and the beast.

Rose and the animal.

Angel and the brute.

Whatever they call us together will be acute,
but all these voices will just be put on mute.

I don't want pressure to make you flee,
I just want this adventure to be about you and me.

Mystery

Deep in the ocean,
there is a mystery,
a semblance of the stare in your soul.

The razor blades of this terrain,
mask our touch to this floor,
which we have set upon.

To our best accord,
can we afford,
for this jury we must adjourn.

Run and Fall

Run and run.

Forever in my heart it will burn.

Like rain,
these futile actions shall disperse into the abyss.

Love however,
will save us all,
from the grasp of this cruel abruption in the wind.

You will run and you will fall,
but my heart will break your fall.

Epiphany

Grey like an ocean,
pray with the motion.

Struggle with faith,
struggle with your heart,
your heart is a hole,
a hole swallowing everything.

Everything in its sight,
everything in the sky.

Everything in the light.

A man will rise,
a man will hide,
bide by lies,
lies like bombs,
scream and shout.

This is your breakthrough,
don't hate through this phase,
for you will face what you have forever wanted to have.

Hail in the sky,
bail from the prison in your life.

For your life will be faced with all the drops of my grace.

A grace I will give you like tears from the sky.

Stand up,
here's the man you want to be,
here's the hay you want to harvest in this monster of a world.

Run like the wind,
I will blow you into the away because far,
far you will go,
with the person who you really are.

Choice

All over my head,
can't go to bed.

Romance is dead,
let's give up instead.

White noise flutters my mind,
these emotions I can't hide.

Am I the bad guy who can't find,
a simple road to guide?

I can't place this mastery,
like an apostrophe,
on a run-on bibliography,
full of atrophy.

Can't make a choice,
gave up my voice,
forehead is moist,
no room to rejoice.

Time is up!

Time to make my choice.

ACT III:

THE ROAD AHEAD

The harmonious crickets that echoed out the emptiness around me.

Supernova

It falls,
bursting with flames.

Agonizing eyes,
red like aged wine.

Let me find your heart,
you precious supernova.

Let me be your platform,
for which you will collide upon this earth,
and upon your arrival it will be me,
who will take the sweet honey fragments of your heart.

Serendipity

Serendipity, they call it,
so I guess I just bought it.

Meteors fly with the glistening flare of your eyes,
poise and strong these temples stand.

Obelisks roam these vast lands,
made from the tears of our fathers,
and the cries of our mothers.

The earth will shatter,
the waves will rise and clash,
and the sky will have us under its foot like a dying roach.

This world will grow old like dying cattle,
but light and beauty coming from you makes this chaos
beautiful.

Serendipity, they call it,
I call it, you.

Honey Tree

Can't get my head right,
this sun shines down so bright.

Stuck in between this crack,
unsure if we will bounce back.

I miss those beautiful eyes,
I wish time would turn counterclockwise.

I'm sorry if I may seem too excessive,
but I can't help staying inexpressive.

Can't wrap my head around this fact,
closest connection I've had has been through physical contact.

Unfortunately, the real message I want to impart,
is that I want to make a home in someone's heart.

Now don't take me wrong,
I'm not here to make you tag along.

Just know that one day,
that wall will have to decay.

I was like a refugee who discovered a new land,
but was thrown out,
when it was starting to become my motherland.

I understand these shoes of fear that you wear,
they made you run away when you were scared.

If no one has ever said this then I will be the first,
you shine a light even when everyone is at their worst.

Only reason my heart hasn't ripped out of my chest,
is because God is holding it with his hands like a nest.

Wish I knew what to expect,
I don't know what will come next.

This isn't some story from one of your books,
this is one of those journeys,
where you'll log the memories into your scrapbook.

Once again, I will remind you,
this message is not to make you blue.

I don't say these words to make you stick with me,
It's just a reminder than your more valuable than a honey tree.

Hearts

To this day,
I search the internet for a chance to see her.

Wondering what those eyes would say,
if they see how I've grown.

Exploiting the ache that still lingers in my heart,
after all these years.

I'd be a liar if I said I didn't want another chance.

Then again calling me a liar would be the polite.

We contemplate about the abstracts of a woman's heart,
how the depths of their feelings go beyond a man's
understanding.

It's unfortunate in our species,
that a man's heart is never explored.

I sat down once with a gay friend of mine,
although we were in some way similar,
if you believe in things being black or white,
we were so different.

His heart was complex too.

To his surprise,
mine was a far reach for him.

Wonder

Science will tell us that our bodies adjust for survival,
it'll ask more when in need,
ask for less when much is given.

So then why do we question,
when the heart looks for freedom,
when the mind looks for relief.

Are we deaf to the signs in front us?

That dare say,
go yonder and ponder,
the dreams that we wonder.

Look at the sky,
for as vast as it seems,
we are brighter than thee.

Butterfly

Oh butterfly,
what brings you to these woods,
uneventful and misunderstood.

Allow me to sit and take in the view,
my eyes have begun to settle on you.

You fly with such particular moves,
of which they will all surely disapprove.

But clearly you must know of this grace,
of which I've begun to embrace.

These melancholy skies,
can't bare your warm blanket eyes.

You should know that your heart,
is something to be earned.

These words may be too far-fetched for someone to listen,
but I must speak on what I have witnessed.

You don't owe me any of your essence,
I am glad to just be in your presence.

Friend

The images that fly,
through the barricades of your vast mind.

Your short blonde curls,
give way to admire the pearls,
that look back at me.

If we were to speak,
we'd probably ignore the world for a week.

Sharing our baggage,
realizing we are just average,
at least that's what we see.

We could gather a band,
but that's not how we feel best in this land.

You bring me warmth as we sit under these trees,
I wish we could freeze,
before we must flee.

So, my friend,
how can we blend,
these feelings we hold before it must end?

Guilty

Why should I feel guilty?

If I believe distance makes the heart grow,
yet you like to smother my space with your thoughts.

Why should I feel guilty?

If I believe God is watching my every step,
yet you act like some sort of lucky charm.

Why should I feel guilty?

If my heart is fond of the beauty in the world,
yet you think you are the best I'll ever have.

Why should I feel guilty?

If I can't tolerate your uproars,
yet you continue until you beat me to submission.

Why should I feel guilty?

If I find solace in the gathering of others,
yet you believe you are all I need to breathe.

Why should I feel guilty?

If I want to conquer this world,
yet you'd like me to lie in chaos.

Why should I feel guilty?

If expressing my peace of mind,
differentiates from what you want me to feel.

Why should I feel guilty?

Of being me,
When you want me to be a distance memory of me.

Who are you?

To make me feel guilty,
Of who I'm becoming.

Romance

What a sight to see.
with your long black hair,
I can't help but remember,
when I would see you push it behind your ears.

The road has been long,
nearly unrecognizable,
yet I can still find you in the masses.

Our paths may never cross again,
my hope is that we have both grown,
from the babes we use to be.

A sight of you is all I need,
to know that you will be free,
of all the mess that crumbles me.

Keep your head up high,
as the moon and sun have their dance.

We may see the same stars in the sky,
in hopes that we may find our romance.

Love Story

I'd like to feel the sky open up,
sunshine pointing at me,
showing me that life is full of wonder.

I'd like to feel the ocean settle,
clear as the skylight glass,
disparaging any faults that I may have.

I'd like to feel the wind cradle me,
shuttering away the quiet,
Giving me sense to the loneliness.

Is it too much to ask,
for a glimpse of what we long?

While we all walk around,
in disbelief that love can't really exist,
we secretly long for that fill.

So, is it too much to ask,
to be honest with ourselves?

To crave our own love story.

Dry Oak

Are some of us without redemption?

Or are we bond to the dry landscape we walk.
byproducts of our circumstances,
or an acquiescent of the choice presented.

Can a Lone Ranger find salt,
in the life he has so chosen to bare?
to be of fire,
or to be of the water that nurtures.

Is this river leading us,
to a cascading tale of deceit.
when will our waterfall come,
to throw us into the deep of calamity.

Are we not human?

Are we not the bare sole,
that set their trace on this kingdom?

How then can we see,
that even a dry oak,
can once again bloom,
with the right season.

Empire

As the house burns down,
a shadow emerges behind it,
with much avail I see its colossal height.

Funny how the crowd disappears,
once my association ends.

Guess that shows the difference,
between friends and acquaintances.

Once the fun is over,
the ants disperse,
with small minds they can't connect.

See I walked around like one of you,
now I see that I was not.

This is my world you see,
my world to live in,
my world to conquer.

For I am not here to build a house,
but to build an empire.

One Last Word:

Regret, like a virus, can slowly break you from the inside. Each day is a new day for a new step. A new step for a new beginning. Don't give up.

www.ingramcontent.com/pod-product-compliance
Lightning Source LLC
Chambersburg PA
CBHW030532130626
46552CB00006B/2223